100 Unforgettable Moments in
The Winter Olympics

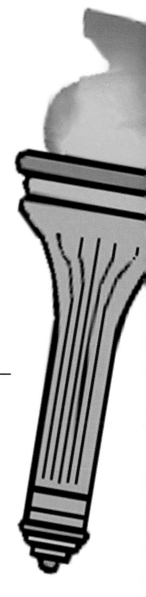

_____

_____

_____

_____

Bob Italia

ABDO & Daughters
Publishing

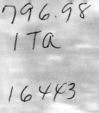

Published by Abdo & Daughters, 4940 Viking Drive,
Suite 622, Edina, Minnesota 55435.

Copyright © 1996 by Abdo Consulting Group, Inc.,
Pentagon Tower, P.O. Box 36036, Minneapolis, Minnesota 55435 USA. International copyrights reserved in all
countries. No part of this book may be reproduced in
any form without written permission from the publisher.

Printed in the United States.

Cover Photo credits: Allsport
Interior Photo credits: Wide World Photo

Edited by Paul Joseph

Library of Congress Cataloging-in-Publication Data

Italia, Bob, 1955-
 100 unforgettable moments in the Winter Olympics /
Bob   Italia.
  p. cm. — (100 unforgettable moments in sports)
 Includes index.
 Summary: Recounts memorable events from past
Winter Olympic games.
 ISBN 1-56239-696-X
  1. Winter Olympics—History—Juvenile literature.
[1. Winter
 Olympics—History. 2. Olympics—History.] I. Title.
II . Series:
 Italia, Bob, 1955-   100 unforgettable moments in
sports.
 GV841.5.I83 1996
 796.98—dc20   96-23093
                                      CIP
                                      AC

Contents

The Most Unforgettable Moment?

The Winter Olympic Games have had many unforgettable moments in their long history. Some of the world's greatest athletes have performed incredible feats and set amazing records. Who could forget the U.S. hockey team's "miracle" victory over the heavily-favored Soviet team in the 1980 Olympics, or speedskater Bonnie Blair's third-successive gold medal in the 500-meter race in 1994?

Some unforgettable moments had nothing to do with world records or superhuman feats. In 1994, Dan Jansen won his one and only Olympic gold medal in men's speed skating. It wasn't the fact that he won which made his performance unforgettable. Rather, it was what he had to endure—and overcome—to win the gold that made his accomplishment so amazing.

There is no one most unforgettable moment in the history of the Olympic Winter Games. The following events are in chronological order, not ranked according to importance. That judgment remains in the hearts of sports fans who have made this worldwide event so special.

Opposite page: Anne Henning, USA speedskater.

Bobsled Billy

William "Billy" Fiske III was a daredevil who loved the bobsled. At the 1928 St. Moritz Olympics, the 16-year-old Fiske was the driver in the four-man bobsled event for the United States team. Fiske led his team to victory—becoming the youngest man to win a gold medal at the Winter Olympics.

Four years later, Fiske carried the American flag in the opening day ceremonies of the Lake Placid Olympic Games. He won his second gold medal driving the four-man sled.

After the Olympics, Fiske joined an international banking firm. He spent half a year in New York and the other in London.

Fiske did not compete at the 1936 Games in Germany. He remained in Great Britain and in 1938 married Rose Bingham, the former Countess of Warwick. Afterward, he was introduced to Air Chief Marshall Sir William Elliot of the Royal Air Force. When World War II began on September 3, 1939, Fiske became a Royal Air Force volunteer and trained as a pilot.

In May 1940, the Battle of Britain began. Twenty-nine-year-old Billy Fiske was now a member of the 601 squadron at Tangmere Airfield near London.

On August 16, 1940, German planes bombed Tangmere's airplanes. Fiske took off and engaged a German bomber in combat. Fiske's engine was hit and his plane caught fire. Fiske landed the plane even though he was badly burned.

Billy Fiske with his wife, Rose Bingham.

Fiske was rushed to the hospital. Though his burns were deep, he was expected to recover. But Billy eventually went into shock and died.

Fiske was given a military funeral in a cemetery outside of London with his squadron comrades as pallbearers. His coffin was draped in British and American flags. Tragically, Fiske had become the first American pilot to be killed in World War II.

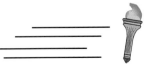

Sonja Henie

Sonja Henie was the greatest influence in women's figure skating. After winning Norway's national championship, 11-year-old Henie competed in the first Winter Olympic Games in 1924, where she finished last.

But in the next four years, Henie prepared for the next Olympics like no other skater before her. During her practice sessions, ballet was combined with pure athletics that would revolutionize the sport. Her program consisted of the kinds of jumps and spins that make up today's best routines. Even more, Henie wore short skirts instead of the usual ankle-length dresses.

The new routine worked wonders. The 14-year-old Henie won her first world championship in 1927. The following year in St. Moritz, she won her first Olympic gold medal.

Henie's success did not end there. At the 1932 Lake Placid Games, she won her second gold medal. She added another world championship before the 1936 Olympics in Garmisch-Partenkirchen, Germany. There, Henie won her third consecutive gold medal—a record that still stands today.

After the 1936 Olympics, Henie turned professional. She also began a career in motion pictures. Henie remains the most commercially successful Olympic champion in history.

Sonja Henie, figure skater and movie star.

9

Birger Ruud's Silver Medal

At the 1932 Winter Olympic Games in Lake Placid, 20-year-old Birger Ruud entered his first Olympic event: the ski jump competition. Because there was very little snow, it had to be trucked in. The jumpers had plenty of snow on the run, but the landing area was a mixture of snow and dirt, making the event difficult.

After the first round, Ruud was in second place. But on his second run, Ruud got off a spectacular leap. With good style points, he won the gold medal.

Two years later, Ruud won the world-famous Holmenkollen ski jump. Already a national hero because of his Olympic medal, Ruud was now a legend.

At the 1936 Winter Games, Ruud entered the 90-meter ski jump competition. If he won the event, Ruud would make Olympic history as the first man to win successive ski jumping gold medals. Ruud did not disappoint himself or his country as he won his second gold medal.

Ruud looked forward to winning the gold again in 1940. But the 1940 and 1944 Games were canceled because of World War II. Ruud was put in jail for two years by the Nazis, who occupied Norway.

When the Winter Games resumed in St. Moritz in 1948, the 36-year-old Ruud was an assistant coach on the Norwegian ski

***The Norwegian ski jump team (left to right), Birger Ruud,
Potter Nugsted, and Throleif Schjelderup.***

jumping team. The night before the games began, the weather
turned foul. Conditions were too dangerous for one of their inex-
perienced jumpers. So Birger Ruud replaced him. In one of the
most remarkable comebacks in Olympic history, Ruud won the
silver medal—12 years after he won his last gold.

The Norwegian team won all three ski-jumping events. But at
the victory platform ceremony honoring the winners, Birger Ruud
received the loudest ovation for his amazing silver-medal
performance.

Andrea Mead Lawrence

One of the most amazing performances in Olympic skiing took place in 1952 at the women's slalom event in Oslo, Norway. There, Andrea Mead Lawrence of the United States performed a feat that may never be matched.

Lawrence had already stunned the skiing world by winning the giant slalom by more than two seconds—a huge margin for a race that is often won by tenths or hundredths of a second. Now Lawrence had a good chance of winning the women's slalom.

At the beginning of the race, Lawrence recorded the fastest time. But in the middle of the course, her ski caught a gate. Before she could stop, she slid past the gate.

After quickly backtracking, Lawrence continued down the course. Lawrence finished the first round in fourth place, 1.2 seconds behind the leader. It looked as though Lawrence was out of gold medal contention.

But on her second attempt, Lawrence flew down the mountain. When the final skier had crossed the finish line, Lawrence had an eight-tenths of a second lead. If she had not missed the gate in her first run, Lawrence would have won by five seconds.

With her remarkable win, Lawrence became the first American ever to win two alpine skiing gold medals.

Andrea Mead Lawrence, Olympic alpine skier.

Sailer's Amazing Sweep

At the 1956 Cortina d'Ampezzo Games in Italy, Austria's Tony Sailer became the first man to win all three alpine skiing events. Sailer's performance was so great, his opponents were skiing for the silver and bronze medals.

In the giant slalom, Sailer won the gold by an amazing 6.2 seconds. Two days later, Sailer entered the slalom event, which consisted of two runs down a winding course. He was the fastest in both runs, and his margin of victory was four full seconds.

The final event was the downhill race. Because of high winds, the course was dangerous. More than one third of the 75 contestants failed to reach the finish line. But Sailer's downhill run was perfect. He won by a huge 3.5-second margin.

Sailer returned to Austria a national hero. Many experts believe his performance in Italy was the greatest in Winter Olympic history.

Opposite page: Austria's Tony Sailer, Olympic downhill skier.

The Amazing Tenley Albright

When Tenley Albright was 11 years old, she contracted polio. She was not completely paralyzed, but she did not have use of her legs and neck. Eventually, she was cured and was able to skate. But the other kids wouldn't play with her, fearing they might catch polio.

At the 1952 Olympics in Oslo, the 16-year-old Albright won a silver medal in women's figure skating. Four years later, she was favored to win the gold at the 1956 Games in Cortina d'Ampezzo, Italy. No American woman had ever won the Olympic figure skating gold medal.

A few weeks before the start of the Cortina Games, tragedy struck. During a practice session, Albright fell and slashed her right leg with the blade of her left skate. Though she got the proper medical treatment, Albright's leg was stiff and her ankle had to be taped on the day of competition.

Albright maintained a slight lead over her teammate, Carol Heiss, after the compulsory exercises. As the freestyle began, Tenley had to perform jumps and spins on her bad leg.

Albright skated to a popular song. Suddenly, the audience began to sing the words, and their voices thrilled her. Albright forgot about her injury and skated flawlessly on her way to the gold medal.

Tenley Albright at Cortina d' Ampezzo, Italy.

That night, Albright stood on the top step of the podium at the medal presentation. Albright's name was announced on the loudspeakers. Then the American flag was raised to the song "My Country 'Tis of Thee." It was the greatest moment of her life.

The Golden Bobsled Driver

In 1954, Eugenio Monti entered a bobsled competition for beginners. His friends decided that he should be the driver. By the time the 1956 Winter Olympics came along, Monti was an expert. He won silver medals in the two-man and four-man events.

Monti had to wait for the 1964 Innsbruck Games to compete again. His two bronze medals were a disappointment. But he earned more honor than if he had won two gold medals.

In the two-man event, the British team led by Tony Nash was in second place after the first run. When they returned to the top of the hill, Nash discovered that his sled had a broken bolt on the rear axle. The breakdown was serious enough to force them from the competition.

At the bottom of the hill, Monti heard of the axle problem. In an amazing act of sportsmanship, Monti took an extra bolt from his rear axle and sent it up to the British team. The British went on to win the gold medal as Monti's team finished third. For his unselfish act, Monti was awarded the De Coubertin Medal for Sportsmanship.

Monti downplayed the entire episode. He did not believe that he did anything that Tony Nash would not have done for him or for anybody else in the competition. "Tony Nash did not win because I gave him a bolt," he said. "Tony Nash won because he was the best driver and deserved to win."

Italian bobsled team led by Eugenio Monti.

Four years later at the 1968 Grenoble Games, Monti was rewarded for his sportsmanship. He won the two-man and four-man events for an Olympic total of two gold, two silver, and two bronze medals.

The Flying Frenchman

Experts consider France's Jean-Claude Killy the greatest all around alpine skier in Olympic history. But at the 1964 Innsbruck Games, Killy competed in all three alpine events—the downhill, slalom, and giant slalom—and did not win a medal. His best showing was a fifth place finish in the giant slalom.

After Innsbruck, Killy improved so much, he became a favorite to medal in all three events at the 1968 Grenoble Games. The downhill race was first.

Killy was the 14th skier. By then, he knew he would have to go all out to win. When Killy finished, the crowd roared as the scoreboard flashed his time. Killy had won by eight hundredths of a second.

The giant slalom event was next. Killy led after the first day, then increased his lead to more than two seconds on the second run for another gold medal.

Finally, it was time for the men's slalom. But the race was held in a thick fog. Killy was in first place after his two runs, but Austria's Karl Schranz had a chance to win the gold with a fast second run. Schranz was on his way to a winning time when suddenly a mysterious figure appeared in his path, forcing him to brake. Schranz protested and was given another chance. This time, he finished ahead of Killy.

Schranz thought he was the winner. But a review board concluded that Schranz had missed two gates on his first run and never should have been given a second chance. He was disqualified and Killy was named the winner.

With the victory, Killy tied Austria's Tony Sailer as the only skiers in Olympic history to win all three men's alpine skiing gold medals in one Olympic event.

Jean-Claude Killy, Olympic alpine skier.

The Perfect Biathlon

The biathlon is one of the most demanding and least known Winter Olympic events. It combines the grueling sport of cross country skiing with the precision of rifle shooting. To win the event, a participant must be a fast skier and an accurate marksman. With each missed target, penalty minutes are added to the cross country time. Even a faster cross country skier can lose if he cannot shoot a rifle accurately.

Magnar Solberg was a police officer in Trondheim, Norway. His superior officer noticed in police training that Solberg was calm under pressure and did not flinch in dangerous situations. Since Solberg was a good cross country skier, he was the perfect candidate for the biathlon.

As the 1968 Grenoble Olympics approached, Solberg went through an intense training program. His shooting routine simulated the stress of Olympic competition.

The most critical times during the competition are the few hundred meters before each shooting phase. Solberg had to concentrate on slowing down his pulse rate at least 50 beats in order to steady his rifle.

At the 1968 Olympics, Solberg was the only athlete to record a perfect "no miss" shooting score. Combined with his second-fastest skiing time, Solberg's marks were good enough to win the gold medal. Four years later in Sapporo, Japan, he defended his Olympic championship.

Magnar Solberg of Norway competing in one of the most demanding Olympic sports—the biathlon.

Miracle on Ice

On February 22, 1980, the young United States hockey team faced the heavily-favored Soviet Union at the Lake Placid Olympic Games. Experts believed that the Soviets had the best hockey team in the world.

Going into the Olympics, the Soviets were ranked first and the United States seventh. In the last six Olympics, the Soviets had won five gold medals and one bronze. Their only loss came 20 years earlier at the 1960 Squaw Valley Olympics when the United States team defeated them in the semifinals.

Amazingly, the Americans played the Soviets tough for two periods. But they still trailed 3-2. Then, nine minutes into the third period, the United States tied the game.

At the 10 minute mark, the "Miracle on Ice" began to take shape. Captain Mike Eruzione blasted 30-foot shot past the stunned Soviet goaltender. The United States led 4-3.

In the final 10 minutes, the Soviets swarmed around the U.S. net. But goalie Jim Craig was brilliant and repelled the furious Soviet attack. Finally, the roaring crowd counted down the last 10 seconds. "Do you believe in miracles?" screamed TV broadcaster Al Michaels. "Yes!"

It was an amazing victory—one of the biggest upsets in Olympic history. But the U.S. team still had to beat the team from Finland to win the gold medal. A silver medal just wouldn't do.

On Sunday, the United States met the Finns and trailed after two periods, 2-1. But this was a game the Americans refused to lose. They scored three goals in the third period and won 4-2. The U.S. had won its second hockey gold medal in 20 years —both coming in the United States.

The miracle on ice—the Americans upset the Soviets.

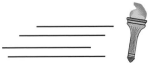

Five for Heiden

At the 1980 Lake Placid Olympics, Eric Heiden of the United States entered all five speed skating races. Experts believed he could win each one.

In the 500-meter race, Heiden was paired with world-record-holder Yevgeny Kulikov of the Soviet Union. After 100 meters, Kulikov was ahead by five-hundredths of a second. But in an electrifying finish, Heiden beat Kulikov by inches.

A third of the way through the 5,000 meters, Heiden was almost five seconds behind Norwegian skater Tom Erik Oxholm. But again, Heiden finished strong for his second gold medal.

Heiden's third race was the 1,000 meters. This time, there was no drama as Heiden won by the huge margin of 1.5 seconds.

Two days later, Heiden's gold-streak continued. He won the 1,500-meter race by more than a second—even though he slipped on a turn.

There was no stopping Heiden now. On the final day of the men's skating competition, Heiden demolished the opposition in the 10,000 meters—breaking the old world record by more than six seconds. The second-place skater finished nearly eight seconds behind. Heiden had done the impossible. He had won five gold medals in five events.

Opposite page:
Speedskater Eric Heiden.

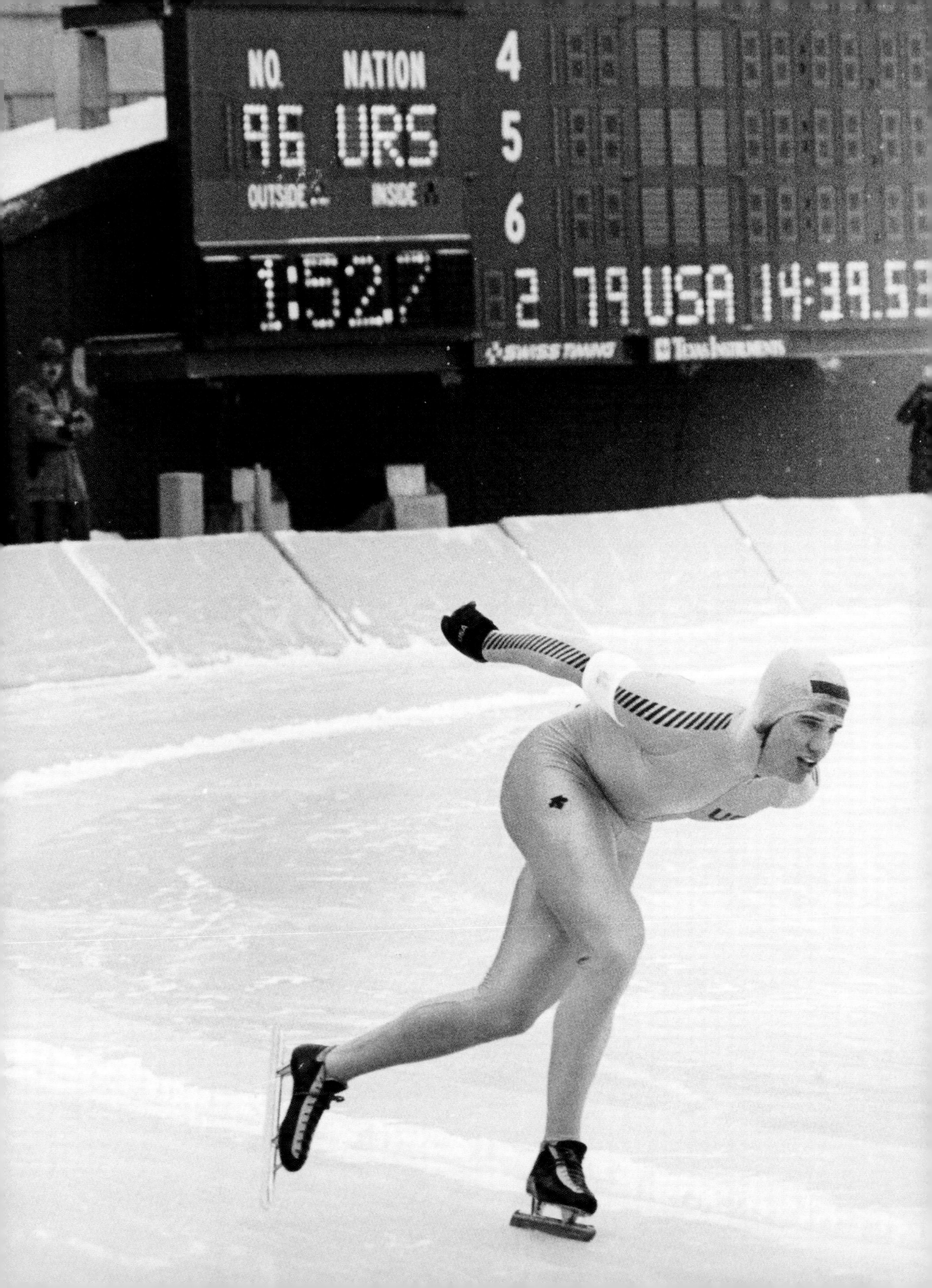
NO. NATION
4
96 URS
5
OUTSIDE INSIDE
6
1:52.7
2 79 USA 14:39.53

Torvill & Dean

When Great Britain's ice dancing team of Jayne Torvill and Christopher Dean finished fifth at the 1980 Lake Placid Games, no one thought they had much of an Olympic future. But following the 1980 Games, they won three world championships—despite painful injuries. Suddenly, Torvill and Dean were overwhelming favorites to win the gold at the 1984 Sarajevo Olympics.

Ice dancing is divided into three separate sessions: two compulsory dances that count for 20% of the final score, original set pattern dance worth 30%, and "free dance" worth 50%.

After the first two sections of competition, Torvill and Dean were far ahead of the competition. If they did not take any risks in the final event, the gold medal was theirs.

But playing it safe did not make Torvill and Dean the greatest ice dancing duo in Olympic history. Skating to Ravel's *Bolero*, Torvill and Dean elevated the sport to new heights with a dazzling display of grace and athleticism. When the scores were flashed for artistic impression, the couple received a perfect six from all nine judges—a mark that may never be reached again.

Jayne Torvill and Christopher Dean of Great Britain at the Olympic Games in Sarajevo, 1984.

The Battle of the Brians

On February 20, 1988, a packed Saddledome in Calgary, Canada, watched the last event of the men's figure skating championship. Although 24 men were entered, everyone knew that the battle for the gold medal would be between Brian Orser of Canada and Brian Boitano of the United States. Orser was the 1987 world champion and silver medalist at the 1984 Sarajevo Olympics. Boitano was the 1986 world champion who finished fifth at Sarajevo.

Boitano led Orser by two-tenths of a point. Each would skate a four-and-a-half-minute long program for the final 50% of their total score.

Boitano skated first—and was nearly flawless. Though Boitano's marks were high, Orser still had the chance to win the gold medal. But Orser needed to skate a perfect program to win.

Each competitor discovered the final result in different ways. Boitano's teammate, Christopher Bowman, ran over to Boitano with a big smile as he nodded his head. Since Bowman was known as a practical joker, Boitano wasn't sure what the final result was.

Brian Orser

"Christopher," Boitano said, "if you're playing a joke on me, it's the meanest thing you've ever done."

"It's no joke," Bowman replied. "You've won!"

Meanwhile, Orser was watching the monitor alongside the Canadian broadcasters. Then he stared at the broadcasters who were giving the results. Orser saw the bleak look on their faces. Then they shook their heads.

The nine judges had given the victory to Boitano by a 5 to 4 decision—the closest finish in Olympic history.

Brian Boitano

Witt Wins Two-in-a-Row

At the 1988 Winter Olympic Games in Calgary, Canada, defending champion Katarina Witt of East Germany won the Olympic gold medal in women's figure skating.

American Debi Thomas had the chance to grab the gold after Witt's freestyle long program did not captivate the judges. But Thomas made four mistakes on jump landings and had to settle for the bronze medal.

Elizabeth Manley of Canada won the long program and earned the silver medal, even though she twice failed to complete her planned triple revolution jumps. Manley became the first woman to defeat Witt in a long program since 1983.

With her gold medal win, Witt joined Sonja Henie of Norway as the only women to win more than one Olympic figure skating title. Henie won three from 1928 to 1936.

"This medal means a lot to me because I am now the second to have more than one," Witt said. "I think it will be a long time before another woman does it."

Opposite page: Katarina Witt of East Germany holds her hands together after finishing her short program at the 1988 Winter Olympics.

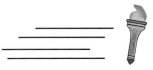

Freestyle Gold

The American skiers had taken a beating in the 1992 Winter Olympics at Albertville, France. But in their best day, Donna Weinbrecht skied through near-blizzard conditions to win the gold medal in the women's freestyle mogul event. With teammate Nelson Carmichael adding a bronze for the men that same day, the U.S. suddenly had two medals in a sport that was just added to the Olympic schedule.

Freestyle skiing had been performed by daredevil American skiers for the past decade. U.S. officials worked hard behind the scenes to interest other nations in the sport. Their efforts paid off in 1992.

Few U.S. athletes had to perform under more pressure than Weinbrecht. She was America's best hope for an Olympic gold medal in skiing for over a year. The 26-year-old New Jersey native had been the reigning world champion in moguls—the only one of three freestyle events that gained Olympic medal status in 1992.

After the previous day's preliminary races, Weinbrecht trailed rival and friend Raphaelle Monod of France. Now she stared down a 250-meter slope lined with 20,000 screaming fans as loud music blared over the public address system.

Weinbrecht's "conservative" effort—judged for speed, difficulty of jumps and style at turning through moguls—gave her 23.69 points. Her score moved her ahead of 18-year-old Elizaveta Kojevnikova of the Unified Team, who had posted a 23.50.

**Donna Weinbrecht competes in the
women's freestyle moguls.**

Now it was Monod's turn. Her speed gave her an edge over
Weinbrecht's athleticism. Midway through her run, she began
drifting off line, righted herself—then went out of control before
tumbling to the snow. The competition was over. Donna
Weinbrecht had won the first-ever gold medal in women's freestyle
mogul event.

Tomba's Last Hurrah

At the 1988 Calgary Olympics, 21-year-old Alberto Tomba of Italy became an instant celebrity by winning the men's slalom and giant slalom events. Four years later in Albertville, Tomba made Olympic history when he won the giant slalom for the second consecutive time—the only alpine skier ever to accomplish this feat. A few days later, Tomba won the silver in the slalom.

In the 1994 Lillehammer Games, 61 men entered the giant slalom event. Not surprising, the 27-year-old Tomba was favored to win his third straight gold medal. But after the first run, Tomba was in 13th place—more than a second behind the leader.

Tomba's fans knew their hero could still win on the second run. Tomba attacked the course with a fury—but missed the third gate from the finish. Tomba was disqualified, and his medal streak was broken.

Four days later, Tomba was the first man down the slalom run. When the 60th skier had crossed the finish line, Tomba was in 12th place—almost two seconds behind the leader.

Tomba had no choice but to attack the course again. This time, Tomba was the only man to reach the finish line under one minute.

Now Tomba had to watch his challengers from the bottom of the hill as they took a run at his electrifying time. One by one, they either failed to finish the course or their times were slower. Amazingly, Tomba was in the lead. Only one skier remained: Austria's Thomas Stangassinger.

Alberto Tomba drives past a gate
in the 1994 Winter Olympics.

Stangassinger skied well and finished the run. Though he was more than a second and a half slower than Tomba, his combined total gave him the victory by 15-hundredths of a second. Tomba could only smile and congratulate the winner.

"It was very exciting to go from twelfth place to second," Tomba said. "And the fact that I won medals at three Olympic Games is something that has never been done in my sport. What more could I ask?"

Smirnov's Journey

Vladimir Smirnov had an unusual journey throughout his Olympic career. At the 1988 Calgary Games, he represented the Soviet Union and won three medals in men's cross-country skiing. Four years later in Albertville, he was part of the Unified Team of the former Soviet republics. Now at the 1994 Lillehammer Games, Smirnov represented his home country of Kazakhstan.

On February 27, Smirnov entered the 50K race. It was the final cross-country event of the Olympics—and Smirnov's last chance for a gold medal. Smirnov had never won an Olympic 50K. He often faded toward the end. Even worse, he would be facing some of the greatest Norwegian skiers of all time.

At every checkpoint, Smirnov had the fastest time. With 10 kilometers left in the race, Smirnov did not slow down. When he entered the stadium, the crowd knew that the gold medal was his.

Because of Smirnov's victory, the national anthem of Kazakhstan was played for the first time in Olympic history.

***Vladimir Smirnov drives towards the
finish line at the 1994 Winter Olympics.***

Koss Is Boss

At the 1994 Lillehammer Games in Norway, experts doubted whether 25-year-old speedskater Johann Olav Koss would be much of a force in the Olympics. Koss had been suffering from a knee injury, and no one knew how he would perform. But in the 5,000-meter race, Koss won the gold medal while setting a world record.

Three days later, Koss entered the 1,500-meter race where he was a big underdog. Experts had ranked him sixth in the world in this event. But Koss surprised everyone when he broke the world record and won the gold.

Four days after his stunning 1,500-meter victory, Koss prepared for the 10,000-meter race. This time, he was a huge favorite to win the gold. Koss had held the world record in this event for more than three years.

Twelve thousand spectators packed the Viking Ship Arena to watch Koss skate. By now, he was one of the biggest stars of the Games. Banners with the words "Koss is Boss" hung everywhere. Finally, Koss' name was announced. Thousands of Norwegian flags waved in salute as the crowd roared.

Koss did not disappoint his fans. By the time he crossed the finish line, Koss had broken his own world record by an incredible 13 seconds!

Three golds in three events. No doubt about it—Koss was boss.

Johann Olav Koss in the 10,000-meter race at the 1994 Winter Olympics.

De Zolt Shows the Way

The men's 4 x 10 kilometer cross-country relay race was an important one to Norway. Leading to the 1994 Games at Lillehammer, the Norwegians had overwhelmed the Olympic competition. In the 1992 Games in Albertville, France, Norway won all five men's cross-country events—including the relay. At Lillehammer, they won the first three men's events. Now they had eight successive victories in two Olympics. A victory in the relay would make it nine in a row. Only Italy and Finland had enough talent to upset the Norwegians.

The 4 x 10 kilometer relay was a team event. A member of each team began the race at the starting line. The winner was the first to cross the finish line. The race was not decided by time.

The first leg was the most important part of the race for the Italian team. They hoped that 43-year-old Maurilio De Zolt could give his team a boost by seizing a quick lead.

De Zolt began his Olympic career at the 1980 Lake Placid Games when he was 29. He won silver medals in the 50-kilometer races in the Calgary and Albertville Games.

De Zolt had a difficult task in the relay. He had to ski against Sture Sivertsen of Norway—the 10K world champion. Even worse, the 10K was not De Zolt's favorite race. Sivertsen had already beaten De Zolt before in the relay event at the World Championships. His margin of victory was more than one minute.

At the start of the race, Norway, Finland, and Italy left the competition behind. At the first passoff, Norway and Finland

battled for the lead. Amazingly, De Zolt was in third place, only 10 seconds behind.

De Zolt's performance kept the Italians in the race—and inspired his teammates. For the rest of the race, the three teams remained within a few feet of each other.

On the last leg, Bjorn Daehlie of Norway raced against Italy's Silvio Fauner. Daehlie had won five gold medals in Albertville and Lillehammer. But Fauner was not intimidated. He was an outstanding sprinter. If he could maintain his fast pace, he had the chance to win the race for Italy.

With 100 meters remaining, Fauner inched into the lead. Repeatedly, Daehlie tried to pass him. But each time Daehlie made his charge, Fauner answered him with a burst of energy. When Fauner was the first to cross the finish line, Italy broke Norway's gold medal streak at eight. More importantly, they were Olympic champions.

Bjorn Daehlie comes up short as Italy breaks Norway's gold medal streak.

Though Fauner's victorious duel over Daehlie was important, the Italian team knew where the race was won. If it wasn't for Maurilio De Zolt, the gold medal would have been lost.

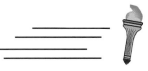

Bonnie Blair

When she was 19 years old, speedskater Bonnie Blair competed in the Olympics for the first time. At the 1984 Sarajevo Games, she finished eighth in the 500-meter race. Though disappointed, Blair did not give up her dream of winning a gold medal. She began preparing for the 1988 Winter Games in Calgary, Canada.

At the Calgary 1988 Games, Blair faced the seemingly unbeatable East German squad, many of whom were defending gold medal champions and held world records.

In the 500-meter race, East Germany's Christa Rothenburger broke her own world record. She seemed a sure bet to successfully defend the title she won four years earlier in Sarajevo. But minutes later, Blair shocked the skating world as she broke Rothenburger's record by two hundredths of a second. Suddenly, the East Germans didn't seem so unbeatable.

Four years later in Albertville, France, Blair successfully defended her title in the 500-meter race by winning the gold, then won her third career gold medal by taking the 1,000-meter race.

At the 1994 Lillehammer Games, Blair had the chance to make Olympic history. If she won the 500 meters, Blair would become the first speedskater—male or female—to win three successive gold medals in the same event.

Blair would not be denied her place in the history books. She skated the race of her life and won her third successive 500-meter gold medal. A few days later, she defended her title in the 1,000 meters, giving her five gold medals overall. It was the last race of her Olympic career.

Bonnie Blair, Olympic speed skating champion.

Picabo's Silver

Picabo Street of Sun Valley, Idaho, scored a big upset in women's alpine skiing when she won a silver medal in the women's downhill at the 1994 Winter Olympics in Lillehammer.

An Olympic medal was something new for the 22-year-old Street, whose parents got her name from a Native American tribe in Idaho. "This is becoming the best day of my life," said Street, whose first name (pronounced "PEEK-uh-boo") translates as "shiny waters."

With the help of Street's performance, American skiers continued to baffle the experts and frustrate onetime alpine skiing powers. Street's medal raised the U.S. alpine totals to four medals—two gold, two silver—in four races. Her performance was not surprising to those who knew her. Street had won the silver medal in the 1993 world championships.

Street raced after Katja Seizinger of Germany who had recorded the best time of the day. Flying down the hill faster than she had expected, Street grew nervous, finishing at 1:36.59.

"That's where I lost a few tenths," said Street.

Although she established herself as an Olympic hopeful while a teenager, Street struggled during a rebellious phase in 1990. She was eventually sent home from training camp with the U.S. junior team because of a temperamental attitude.

Soon after leaving the team, Street joined her family in Maui, Hawaii. Her father told her, "You're a world-class athlete. You should at least give it a shot. Go ahead and play this thing out."

Her father pushed her to train every day. He clocked her sprints and screamed at her to complete her exercises. Street fought him all the way.

"Hate me now," he said. "Thank me later."

Eventually, Street decided what was important to her. "I sat down and wrote the pros and cons of being a ski racer," she said, "and the pros way outweighed the cons, so I buckled down. My dad stayed on top of me for three months and trained me hard."

It paid off for Street as she took home the silver medal.

Picabo Street streaks over the course at the Winter Olympics, 1994.

Norway Returns

In the early years of the Olympics, Norway dominated ski jumping. But since 1964, the country had not won a gold medal in this popular event. Then the 1994 Lillehammer Games came along. And so did Epsen Bredesen.

Norway pinned their ski jumping hopes on Bredesen in the 120-meter event. After a last-place finish in the 1992 Olympics in Albertville, France, Bredesen won 10 of 14 events before the 1994 Winter Games. Norway had finally found a hero. Even the king and queen had come to watch Bredesen jump.

With their country's red-and-blue flags waving throughout the stadium, thousands cheered Bredesen's first jump—a stadium-record 135.5 meters.

Rock music boomed through loudspeakers as Bredesen prepared for his final jump. The Norwegians roared with gold-medal anticipation as Bredesen began his long slide down the jump. But a poor takeoff hurt his chances for another outstanding score. When Bredesen landed well short of his first mark, the crowd had already faded into an eerie silence. Bredesen's poor second jump knocked him to second place, allowing Germany's Jens Weissflog to win the gold for the second consecutive time.

Bredesen's last chance for a gold medal—and redemption—came in the 90-kilometer jump. Bredesen did not let his country down as he set an Olympic record with 282 points. Once again, the flags waved and the music boomed. After a long drought, Norway finally got its ski jumping gold medal.

Epsen Bredesen soars through the air at the 1994 Winter Olympics.

Moe's Golden Victory

At the 1994 Winter Games in Lillehammer, Norway's Kjetil Andre Aamodt had just finished his magnificent run in the men's downhill when American Tommy Moe positioned himself at the starting gate. Moe wasn't given much of a chance to win the gold. The 30,000 local fans were already celebrating Aamodt's apparent victory. Even Moe wasn't convinced he could win. Throughout his Olympic career, he had disappointed himself with less-than-spectacular runs. Critics assumed that the U.S. alpine team would fail again in Lillehammer.

Two years earlier on the slopes of Val d'Isere in France, Moe finished a disappointing 20th in the Olympic downhill. Frustrated with the performance, Moe's father lashed back at his son. With tears in his eyes, Tommy Moe skied away. It wasn't the first time Moe and his father were at odds.

When he was 16 years old, Moe was kicked off the U.S. alpine team. His father brought Moe to Dutch Harbor, off the Aleutian Islands in Alaska. Moe worked construction 12 hours a day under the watchful eye of a father determined to set his son straight.

"I hammered him," Tom Moe said. "Anything I could do to burn him to the ground. I wanted him to hate it. And I made him hate it. He made the right choice. I didn't have to make it for him."

All the hard work and guidance paid off. Moe's 1:45.75 beat Aamodt's time of 1:45.79 by .04 seconds—and buried years of

frustration. The victory gave the U.S. its first downhill gold medal since 1984, when Bill Johnson won at Sarajevo.

"The biggest surprise was when I came down and I was in first," said the 23-year-old Moe. "I was pretty excited. I took my skis off and I thought, 'Hey, I might be there for a medal today.' That was my main concern, getting any color medal."

When he realized he had won, Moe grabbed a U.S. flag and another from his home state of Alaska. Then Moe and his father shared a moment of personal satisfaction as they embraced.

Tommy Moe goes airborne during the men's downhill at the 1994 Winter Olympics.

Baiul's Moment of Glory

At the 1994 Winter Games in Lillehammer, Norway, 16-year-old Oksana Baiul of Ukraine was in second place in women's figure skating and within striking distance of the leader, America's Nancy Kerrigan. But no one knew if Baiul could compete in the finals. The day before, she collided with another skater during a practice session and suffered back and leg injuries. Her pain was so great, she needed painkilling drugs.

Pain was not new to Baiul. Her father left home when she was very young. When Baiul was 13 years old, her mother died of cancer. Baiul moved in with her grandparents, but they died shortly after. When she was 15, Baiul had to say good-bye to her coach of 9 years, who moved to Canada.

Then skater Viktor Petrenko came along. Petrenko was the 1992 Albertville gold medal winner. He asked his coach and mother-in-law, Galina Zmievskaya, to take Baiul into her home. So she became a member of the family—and Zmievskaya became her coach. Baiul flourished under Zmievskaya's watchful eye, and became a gold-medal contender.

In the Lillehammer finals, Kerrigan skated before Baiul. Many thought she gave a gold medal performance. But Baiul still had a chance to win. Baiul's first jump—a difficult triple lutz—was flawless. It was the first of five triple jumps she would execute to perfection.

When Baiul finished her routine, the crowd gave her a standing ovation. Now she had to wait for her scores. Four of the nine

Oksana Baiul reacts after her performance at the Olympics.

judges gave their first place votes to Baiul. The other four voted for Kerrigan. The ninth judge called it a tie.

According to the rules, the artistic score becomes the tie-breaker. Since Baiul was a 10th of a point higher than Kerrigan in that category, she became the gold medal winner.

For the first time in Olympic history, the Ukrainian national anthem was played at the medals presentation.

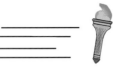

The Saga of Dan Jansen

At the 1988 Winter Games in Calgary, Canada, speedskater Dan Jansen of the United States was favored to win the 500- and 1,000-meter races. But the rigors and pressure of Olympic competition were nothing compared to the personal tragedy he was about to face. His beloved sister Jane was dying of leukemia.

On the morning of the 500 meters, Jansen's mother called her son and told him that Jane probably wouldn't make it through the day. Jansen talked to his sister one last time and promised to win the race for her. Jane couldn't talk, but understood what Jansen was saying. Three hours later, Jane died.

Hours before his first race, Jansen practiced grimly on the Olympic oval. His thoughts took him far away from Calgary. At the beginning of the 500-meter race, Jansen got off to a fast start. But less than 100 meters later, he slipped and fell to the ice. For Jansen, the race was over.

Four days later in the 1,000-meter race, Jansen was on his way to a record-breaking performance. But then, with one lap to go, he slipped and fell. For the second time, Jansen failed to finish a speed skating race he was expected to win.

At the 1992 Albertville Games, Jansen was favored to win both speed skating events. But for some reason, Jansen could not realize his Olympic-medal dreams. He finished fourth in the 500 meters, and 26th in the 1,000 meter race.

Jansen decided to give it one more try at the 1994 Lilleham-mer Games. By then, he was the world record holder in the 500 meters—and the only skater to finish under 36 seconds.

Jansen started off quickly in the 500 meters. In the stands, his wife Robin cheered every powerful stride, while Robin's mother held the Jansens' nine-month-old daughter, Jane. She was named after Dan's sister, who had died six years ago to the day.

Dan Jansen, Olympic speedskater, sets a new world's record.

Jansen was flying around the oval. But then on the last turn, he slipped. This time, Jansen maintained his balance and finished the race. But the slip cost him a medal as he finished in eighth place.

Four days later, Jansen entered the last race of his Olympic career. It was the 1,000 meters. Jansen was not confident, and didn't feel good about his chances. Besides, his skates weren't gripping the ice properly. "All I could think of was 'this will be over soon,' " Jansen said. " 'In a minute and a half, it will be done.' "

With his confidence shaken, Dan Jansen skated the greatest race of his Olympic career—despite a slip on the next to last turn. When he crossed the finish line, Jansen broke the world record by 11-hundredths of a second.

Standing on the victory platform, Jansen's mind drifted once again. "I was hoping the national anthem would never end," he said. "My whole life passed by me: my family, Robin, my daughter Jane—and, of course, my sister Jane. As the anthem was nearing its end, I was trying to think of saying something to Jane. So I looked up and gave a little salute." The Dan Jansen saga had begun with her death. Now it could finally end.

After the medal ceremony, Jansen took a victory lap. As he glided around the track, Jansen stopped at the stands to gather his daughter in his arms. Smiling with satisfaction, Jansen carried Jane around the oval. Thousands cheered as they said goodbye to this courageous athlete.

Opposite page: Dan Jansen exults after winning the gold medal.

More Unforgettable Moments

1928—Clas Thunberg wins his second consecutive gold medal in the men's 1500-meter speed skating event.

1928—Gillis Grafstrom wins his third consecutive gold medal in men's figure skating.

1928—Bernt Evensen sets an Olympic record in the men's 500-meter speed skating event.

1932—Canada wins its fourth consecutive gold medal in ice hockey.

1932—Johan Grottumsbraaten wins his second consecutive gold medal in the nordic combined event.

1932—John Shea sets an Olympic record in the men's 500-meter speed skating event.

1936—Birger Ruud wins his second consecutive gold medal in the 90-meter ski jump.

1936—Ivar Ballangrud sets an Olympic record in the men's 10,000-meter speed skating event.

1936—Great Britain upsets Canada to win the gold medal in ice hockey.

1936—Karl Schafer wins his second consecutive gold medal in men's figure skating.

1936—Ivar Ballangrud sets an Olympic record in the men's 500-meter speed skating event.

1936—Charles Mathisen sets an Olympic record in the men's 1500-meter speed skating event.

1936—Ivar Ballangrud sets an Olympic record in the men's 5000-meter speed skating event.

1948—Finn Helgesen sets an Olympic record in the men's 500-meter speed skating event.

1948—Sverre Farstad sets an Olympic record in the men's 1500-meter speed skating event.

1952—Dick Button wins his second consecutive gold medal in men's figure skating.

1952—Hjalmar Andersen sets Olympic records in the men's 5000-meter and 10,000-meter speed skating events.

1956—The Soviet Union hockey team defeats Canada for the gold.

1956—Sigvard Ericsson sets an Olympic record in the men's 10,000-meter speed skating event.

1956—Hallgeir Brenden wins his second consecutive gold medal in the men's 15-kilometer nordic skiing event.

1956—Yevgeny Grishin and Yuri Mikhailov set a world record in the men's 1500-meter speed skating event.

1956—Boris Shilkov sets an Olympic record in the men's 5000-meter speed skating event.

1960—The U.S. team upsets Canada to win the gold medal in ice hockey.

1960—Yevgeny Grishin wins his second consecutive gold medal in the men's 500-meter speed skating event.

1960—Knut Johannesen sets the world record in the men's 10,000-meter speed skating event.

The U.S. celebrates their upset over Canada.

1964—Lydia Skoblikova wins her second consecutive gold medal in the women's 1500-meter speed skating event.

1964—Terry McDermott sets an Olympic record in the men's 500-meter speed skating event.

1964—Lydia Skoblikova sets an Olympic record in women's 500-meter speed skating event.

1964—Knut Johannesen sets an Olympic record in the men's 5000-meter speed skating event.

1968—Cornelis Verkerk sets an Olympic record in the men's 1500-meter speed skating event.

1968—Fred Anton Maier sets a world record in the men's 5000-meter speed skating event.

1968—Eugenio Monti wins two gold medals in bobsledding.

1968—Lyudmila Beloussova and Oleg Protopopov win their second consecutive gold medal in mixed pairs figure skating.

1968—Johnny Hoglin sets an Olympic record in the men's 10,000-meter speed skating event.

1972—Anne Henning sets an Olympic record in the women's 500-meter speed skating event.

1972—Erhard Keller wins his second consecutive gold medal in the men's 500-meter speed skating event.

1972—Ard Schenk sets an Olympic record in the men's 1500-meter speed skating event.

1976—The USSR wins its fourth consecutive gold medal in ice hockey.

1976—Yevgeny Kulikov sets an Olympic record in the men's 500-meter speed skating event.

1976—Sheila Young sets an Olympic record in the women's 500-meter speed skating event.

1976—Jan Egil Storholt sets an Olympic record in the men's 1500-meter speed skating event.

1976—Piet Kleine sets an Olympic record in the men's 10,000-meter speed skating event.

1980—Ingemar Stenmark wins two gold medals in men's skiing.

1980—Hanni Wenzel wins two gold medals in women's skiing.

1980—East Germany wins its fourth consecutive gold medal in men's doubles luge.

1980—Karin Enke sets an Olympic record in the women's 500-meter speed skating event.

1980—Irina Rodnina and Aleksandr Zaitzev win their third consecutive gold medal in mixed pairs figure skating.

1980—Leonhard Stock sets the Olympic record in the men's downhill.

1980—Ulrich Wehling wins his third consecutive gold medal in the nordic combined event.

1984—Karin Enke sets the world record in the women's 1500-meter speed skating event.

1984—Nikolai Simyatov wins his second consecutive gold medal in the men's 30-kilometer nordic skiing event.

1988—Matti Nykanen wins his second consecutive gold medal in the men's large hill ski jumping event.

1988—Alberto Tomba wins two gold medals in men's downhill skiing.

1988—Sigrid Wolf of Austria sets the Olympic record in the women's super giant slalom while capturing a gold medal.

Sigrid Wolf shows her golden smile.

1988—Nikolai Gulyaev sets an Olympic record in the men's 1000-meter speed skating event.

1988—Andre Hoffman sets a world record in the men's 1500-meter speed skating event.

1988—Yvonne van Gennip sets world records in the women's 3000-meter and 5000-meter speed skating events.

1988—The men's 4 x 7.5-kilometer relay team from the Soviet Union wins its 6th consecutive gold medal in the biathlon.

1988—Steffi Walter wins her second consecutive gold in the women's singles luge.

1988—Ewe-Jens Mey sets the world record in the men's 500-meter speed skating event.

1988—Bonnie Blair sets the world record in the women's 500-meter speed skating event.

1988—Christa Rothenburger sets a world record in the women's 1000-meter speed skating event.

1988—Tomas Gustafson sets a world record in the men's 5,000-meter and 10,000-meter speed skating events.

1992—Ewe-Jens Mey wins his second consecutive gold medal in the men's 500-meter speed skating event.

1992—Kim Ki-Hoon sets the world record in the men's 1000-meter short track speed skating event.

1992—Kjetil Andre Aamodt sets the Olympic record for the men's super giant slalom.

1994—Aleksandr Golubev sets the Olympic record in the men's 500-meter speed skating.

1994—The men's 5000-meter relay team sets an Olympic record in the short track speed skating.

1994—The women's short track speed skating team from South Korea sets the Olympic record in the 3000-meter relay.

1994—The men's 4 x 7.5-kilometer relay team from Germany wins its 2nd consecutive gold medal in the biathlon.

1994—Switzerland wins its second consecutive gold medal in the two-man bobsled.

1994—Georg Hackl wins his second consecutive gold medal in the men's singles luge.

1994—Bjorn Daehlie wins his second consecutive gold medal in the men's 15-kilometer freestyle nordic skiing event.

1994—Japan wins its second consecutive gold medal in the team nordic combined event.

1994—Lyubov Egorova wins her second consecutive gold medal in the women's 10-kilometer freestyle pursuit event.

Index